ALL ABOARD AMERICA

Jamestown

ABDO
Publishing Company

A Buddy Book
by
Sarah Tieck

VISIT US AT
www.abdopublishing.com

Published by ABDO Publishing Company, 8000 West 78th Street, Edina, Minnesota 55439.

Copyright © 2008 by Abdo Consulting Group, Inc. International copyrights reserved in all countries. No part of this book may be reproduced in any form without written permission from the publisher. Buddy Books™ is a trademark and logo of ABDO Publishing Company.

Printed in the United States.

Contributing Editor: Michael P. Goecke
Graphic Design: Deborah Coldiron
Cover Photograph: North Wind Picture Archives
Interior Photographs/Illustrations: National Geographic Photography (pages 19); North Wind Picture Archives (pages 7, 11, 13, 15, 17, 21, 22); Photos.com (page 9)

Library of Congress Cataloging-in-Publication Data

Tieck, Sarah, 1976–
    Jamestown / Sarah Tieck.
       p. cm. — (All aboard America)
    Includes bibliographical references and index.
    ISBN 978-1-59928-936-6
    1. Jamestown (Va.)—History—Juvenile literature. I. Title.

F234.J3T54 2008
973.2'1—dc22

2007027265

Table of Contents

Jamestown is important to U.S. history. Many say it is where America began.

The first settlers reached Jamestown in 1607. It became the **New World's** first English settlement.

Many times before, English people had tried to settle in the New World. But, Jamestown was the first settlement to survive.

Today, Jamestown is a valuable **resource**. **Archaeologists** study it to learn about America's beginnings.

In the 1600s, England and Spain were fighting to claim the New World. Many people think America began when the pilgrims landed at Plymouth Rock in 1620. Others say it began 13 years earlier, in Jamestown.

About 104 men and boys were Jamestown's first settlers. They arrived in three boats provided by an English company.

As they traveled through swampy waters, they saw strawberry plants and cedar and cypress trees. The land was wild and unsettled.

The group chose a site and set up camp. It was on a hill overlooking a river. Later, the English settlers would name the settlement Jamestown for their king, James I.

Jamestown was located on what is now known as the James River. Back then, the settlement was spelled "Jamestowne."

Jamestown was located in Virginia swampland. When the settlers first arrived, they spent a few days unpacking. Then, the settlement leaders explored the area.

Shortly after arriving, the settlers were attacked by Native American tribes. So, they built a triangle-shaped fort for protection. The fort's walls wrapped around the settlement.

John Smith was both liked and hated as a Jamestown leader. Still, he helped the settlement in many ways. For example, he traded for food with the Native Americans.

Inside Jamestown's walls the settlers constructed many buildings. There were houses and workshops. The settlers stayed very busy!

They made many buildings by packing mud and straw into wooden frames. Each building had several fireplaces and rooms.

The settlers also dug a well for drinking water. And, they built **palisades** for protection.

About half of Jamestown's early residents were rich gentlemen. Others were craftsmen and laborers. All of them had to work very hard to survive.

Daily life in Jamestown brought many challenges. Native Americans made many attacks. The settlers fought with each other, too. Also, a **drought** made food hard to find and grow.

The settlers had to find ways to survive in the **New World**. Sometimes they traded with the Native Americans. Other times, they received food from England. Still, they often had nothing to eat.

The settlers made some Native American friends. Chief Powhatan's daughter Pocahontas was one of them. She was a friend to John Smith. Later, she married Jamestown settler John Rolfe.

During the first few years, hundreds more people arrived in Jamestown. However, about 400 of them died. The colony suffered sickness, hunger, attacks, accidents, and bad weather.

A Turning Point

By 1610, only 60 Jamestown settlers remained alive. Many settlers had died during "The Starving Time." The area had undergone a long **drought**. So, the people had run out of food and were eating anything they could find.

The settlers decided to leave for England. But as they were sailing away, help came! Lord De La Warr arrived with a ship carrying food and supplies.

This English **aristocrat** proved to be a strong leader. He helped the settlers rebuild their settlement, and Jamestown was saved.

Lord De La Warr arrived with supplies and new settlers. He helped save Jamestown.

In its later years, Jamestown became very successful. Eventually, more than 1,000 men and women lived in the flourishing settlement!

In the **New World**, the settlers could easily get important **resources**. They used these to make products to sell in England.

Some settlers worked as tailors. Others made perfume or glass. Some used the land to grow crops, such as tobacco. The settlers also harvested plants that contained medicines.

The Jamestown settlers grew crops and made products. Then, they shipped them to England.

CHAPTER 7

A Historic Search

Eventually, people stopped living in Jamestown. The site was abandoned for many years. In the 1800s, some people even believed the fort had sunk into the river.

But in 1994, **archaeologists** began looking for Jamestown's exact site. They didn't know if the original fort and its buildings could be found. Still, they began **excavating**. They found the fort!

Today, there are more than 500,000 objects from Jamestown for people to see. These **artifacts** teach people about life long ago in the colony.

Some say Jamestown is one of the most important archaeological sites ever discovered. Some artifacts include pottery shards and tobacco pipes.

Detour

Did You Know?

. . . Before Jamestown, settlers tried many times to start settlements in the New World. It was not easy to survive!

. . . In 1889, people believed all that was left of Jamestown was a church tower and some gravestones. The Association for the Preservation of Virginia Antiquities acquired 22 acres (9 ha) near the historic site. It wanted to keep the site safe for future visitors.

. . . For a short time, Jamestown was Virginia's capital. This was where some of the country's first laws were made.

. . . **Archaeologist** Bill Kelso launched the Jamestown Rediscovery Project in 1994. Using his spade, he found the first pieces of the settlement's fort.

Today, archaeologists have found many pieces of the original settlement. There are even remains of some Jamestown homes.

Jamestown Today

Today, Jamestown is an **archaeological** site. It is still considered a very important place in America. Many say it was where our country began!

In 2007, Jamestown turned 400 years old. There was a large celebration at the site.

Archaeologists continue to make new discoveries. They even discovered Jamestown's original well. This helped them learn about life long ago.

Important Words

archaeologist a scientist who studies people and objects from the past.

aristocrat a member of the nobility.

artifact an important object from history.

drought a long period of dry weather.

excavate to dig or uncover.

New World a term explorers used to refer to the Americas.

palisade a protective fence.

resource a supply of something useful.

WEB SITES

To learn more about Jamestown, visit ABDO Publishing Company on the World Wide Web. Web sites about Jamestown are featured on our Book Links page. These links are routinely monitored and updated to provide the most current information available.
www.abdopublishing.com

Index